THE CABIN

Erin Dulhanty Herr

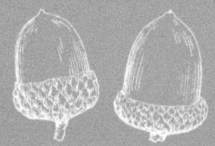

HOG PRESS

Hog Press
918 5th Street
Ames, IA 50010
USA

hogpress.com

editor@hogpress.com

HOG PRESS

THE CABIN
Copyright © 2021 by Erin Dulhanty Herr.
All rights reserved.

No part of this book may be reproduced in any form by any electronic or mechanized means (including photocopying, recording, or information storage and retrieval) without written permission, except in the case of brief quotations embodied in critical articles and reviews.

For more information, please address
editor@hogpress.com

ISBN: 978-1-941892-47-3

Cover design and interior layout © 2021 polytekton

TABLE OF CONTENTS

Preface	5
Winter 1892	13
Spring 1893	17
Summer 1893	21
Fall 1893	25
Winter 1893	29
Spring 1894	33
Summer 1894	37
Fall 1894	41
Enrichment Questions/Activities for Students	44

Herr Family Photo

Northside of Herr cabin

Southside of Herr cabin

Westside of Herr cabin

Preface

Window inside Herr cabin

Fireplace inside Herr cabin

The log cabin in this story sits now in Lebanon Memorial Park in Lebanon, Indiana. It is called Herr Cabin and is used for community events and private functions, but for several generations it was located seven miles south of Lebanon. The characters in this book are some of my husband's ancestors.

Father and Mother are Benjamin Levi Herr and Abigail Davis Herr – my husband, Dave Herr's, great-great grandparents. Charley, John, Nell, and Ben are four of their six children.

Benjamin L. and Abigail bought the log cabin and 160 acres in Perry Township, Boone County, Indiana, on August 9, 1882 for $6,400 from Nicholas Yount, an early settler. Yount had built the two-room cabin in 1839, five and half miles southeast of Lebanon, Indiana.

For twelve years, Benjamin L. and Abigail lived in the cabin and farmed the land. Eventually, their family grew to six children – Charley, John, Nell, Nan, Shirl, and Ben.

In the summer of 1894, the family built and moved into a two-story, ten-room white frame house on a hill a quarter mile north of the cabin.

After Charley married, he moved into the cabin with his wife, Flora. They had a son Garrett, and daughter, Margaret, known as 'Marnie.' Garrett was born in the cabin. Charley and Flora would be the last Herr's to live in it. Eventually they would move to the large white frame house.

Three more generations of Herr's would live in the house built by Benjamin L. and Abigail. They would farm the land, too. Garrett's son Sam, and his wife, Frances Honan Herr, lived in the house for a short time.

Sam and Frances's son, David, my husband, and I lived in the white frame house for two years after our wedding in 1988. By this time, the house was beyond our means to repair it. On April 16, 1990, the day our daughter, Caitlin Elizabeth Herr was born, it was torn down. That summer we built a new farmhouse on the exact spot of the old one, keeping part of the original basement, some of the woodwork, and gingerbread framing around the front porch. Four years later, our son Michael Sam Herr was born, on December 7, 1994.

Herr Elevator Construction

Herr Grain Elevator, Date Unknown

Herr Grain Elevator, 1923

David Herr is the fifth generation Herr to own and farm our land. The farm has continued to grow, and we now farm 1,500 acres. Our son Michael, 26, began farming full time after graduating from college, and is the sixth generation to work and live here. He and his wife, Regan Holtsclaw Herr, live in a home built by Ben Herr. Our daughter, Caitlin Herr, lives in Lebanon.

When I stand in our driveway, I look south down the lane that led to the cabin, barns, and windmill that once stood there long ago. While writing this story I saw our farm, where I have lived now for 33 years, in a new 'old' way. It was fun researching and learning about the lives of my husband's ancestors. Even though they lived and worked here over

John Herr with the Herr Harvester and patent attorney

Herr Grain Elevator, Date Unknown

Clover Harvester Invention

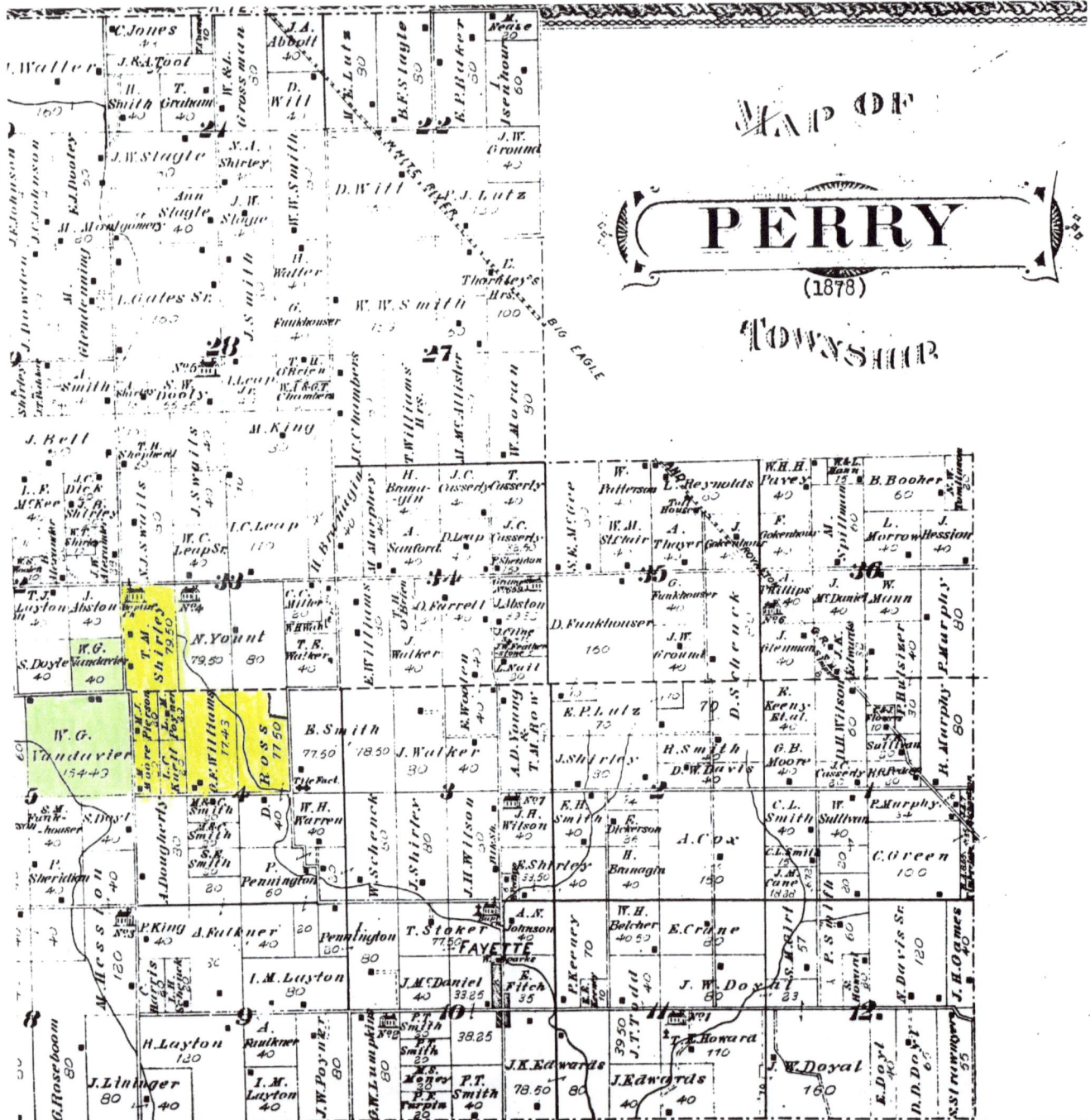

100 years ago, I was struck by the saying, "the more things change, the more they stay the same." While there are many joys to what we do, farming is still tough at times – dealing with unpredictable weather, worries about crops, the safety of our children growing up on a busy farm, as well as grain prices, equipment failures and more. All of this Nell reflected on, too. In her writings, she shared how her parents worried about these very issues. Even though it can be stressful, it is worth continuing the legacy of Herr Farms for the next generations. If we have a good year, fantastic; if we have a bad year, we always look to the next to be better. We would not want to do anything else. Our children have this place - a beautiful, working farm with acres of land and a woodland to always call home, as well as the memories and stories of generations who did the same. I hope it will always be a special place they want to preserve.

The events in this story are true but I did use creative license to imagine their lives here on the farm. I compressed the events, which happened over several years, into three years, although by the late 1890s half of the six Herr children were young adults. Even though Benjamin L. and Abigail had six children, I chose to write about four. Shirl's leg, not John's, was injured by a wagon wheel, and he would limp the rest of his life. The family did their "trading," as it was called, at a store in Fayette but it was not called Leap's General Store. The Leap's were neighbors of the Herr's. John found arrowheads on the farm and, over many years, more would be found, several by Garrett Herr. John was an avid reader, especially about history, and had a book on Egypt that Nell could recall even at 90 years old. John would go on to build and obtain a patent for the Herr Harvester, a horse-drawn clover harvesting machine. Charley, forever the jokester, did put Nell in Father's pants and left her hanging from a rafter in the cabin.

In the winter, the story goes, the Herr children ice skated on the frozen "swamp" ground. They did not have a deep pond on the farm although that area of the farm is still low to this day and water stands on it almost year-round.

Charley dynamited stumps from "Stump Field" so his plowshares would not break on the roots. A neighbor's dog, Old Trail, was beloved by the Herr children and buried on the farm. Old Moll and Old Weasel were the names of two of their horses. The baby of the family, Ben Herr, would grow up to farm, become a state representative and state senator. He was also a pilot, owned a plane, and had an airstrip on the farm. Like John, he had a deep love of history, especially of Boone County and Indiana. In 1917 John and Charles built the Herr Elevator which mixed and ground seed, as well as sold coal, grain for animal feed, and seeds for planting. Later, it became Kern, Kirtley and Herr Grain Elevator, located in what was then known as "Herr Station," and it is still in operation although no longer owned by the Herr family.

So how did the cabin end up in Lebanon Memorial Park? Some records indicate John donated the cabin as a dedication to his mother, possibly because the cabin was dedicated a year or so after her death, but Nell had a different recollection. The following is from a letter she wrote to the editor of the local newspaper correcting an article they had published about the cabin. The year was 1968 and she lived in California.

> In the early 1930s the James Hill Chapter, Daughter of the American Revolution, became hard pressed for a meeting place. My mother, Abigail Herr, a long-time member, offered the deserted cabin. Accepted, it was divested of its weatherboarding, its porch and summer kitchen combination and its two crumbly brick chimneys. Its logs, numbered and disassembled, were reassembled on its present site in Memorial Park in Lebanon. On October 19, 1935 it was dedicated.
>
> Yours respectfully,
> Nell Herr Galey

WINTER 1892

Charley flung open the front door of Mr. Leap's store and shouted, "Father, come quick! John's hurt!" He raced back to the side of the wagon and knelt beside John.

John was lying on his side in the snow, his right leg pulled up to his chest, moaning. "Oh Father, it hurts. It hurts real bad." Tears ran down his red cheeks. Fat snowflakes clung to his hat.

Father turned to Charley, "What happened out here? Were you pestering him again?"

"No sir. I, well, I was moving the wagon around to the side. Old Moll was acting fidgety so I thought it would help. John must have been standing on the wheel when I took off. He got his leg caught in the spokes. I didn't know…" Charley's voice trailed off.

"Fine. We'll talk about it when we're home," Father said.

Father lifted John into the back of the wagon, covering him with a blanket. "Charley, you're going to sit back here and keep him company. John, the ride home won't be a picnic but you be strong for me, okay?"

"Yes sir," John said wiping his nose.

Mr. Leap put the package for Mother next to John. It was her Christmas present – three fine lengths of fabric from New York. And in all of her favorite colors of blue, purple, and green. On their way to Mr. Leap's General Store in Fayette, Father, Charley and John had discussed how she would surely cry when she saw them in the morning. Mother had not had new fabric in a year.

Charley didn't dare say it, but he was fit to be tied at John. Charley was supposed to drive the wagon home. Father had allowed him to take over the job this past fall. If John had not been so careless and jumped when the wagon began moving, Charley thought, none of this would have happened. John sniffled and Charley put his arm around him despite his anger.

The four-mile ride was indeed long for John. The wagon got stuck once in a snowdrift and Charley didn't think he and Father were ever going to get it loose. The ride home stretched to two hours.

When they pulled up to the cabin, Mother raced out with Nell close behind.

"What took you so long?" I was worried sick. Your supper's gone cold..." She looked in the wagon at John.

"Lordy, what happened?" Mother raced over to him.

"My leg. It hurts real bad, Mother," John stammered.

"No time for explanations now. Let's get him inside before we all freeze," Father said hoisting John out of the wagon. The air was full of flying snow and the sky beyond a dizzying white.

Charley climbed onto the seat of the wagon and clucked at Old Moll. He would gladly put him away for the night.

Father set John's broken leg, his screams carried out of the cabin, over the wind, into the barn, where Charley hung his head and wiped a tear onto a sleeve. Mother made John a cup of her home brew of willow bark, cramp bark, and valerian. John finally settled down and fell into a fitful sleep in Mother and Father's bed.

"His leg doesn't look good," Mother said to Father as she handed him a cup of coffee. She adjusted the star on top of the Christmas tree and wiped at her eyes with her shawl. "I don't know if it that leg will ever be right again."

Charley and Nell stood at the doorway of the bedroom. They watched John who was snoring now. Father got up and put his arms around Mother. They stood staring at the Christmas tree for a long time. Charley and Nell quietly settled into their beds for the night.

"Charley, wake up. He's been here!" Nell said.

Charley sat up and shook his head, groggy from tossing and turning all night. "Who's been here?" Is John okay?"

"Santa, silly!" Nell said. "John's out here. Come on. See what Santa left us."

Around the tree sat new shoes for Charley, John and Nell. An orange and some brightly-wrapped candy were tucked in each.

"We were waiting on you sleepyhead," Mother said. "Okay, you can pick them up now." Nell raced to her shoes. New hair ribbons!

Charley picked up John's shoes. He carried them over to the kitchen table where John sat his bandaged leg propped on the bench.

"Sorry about yesterday. I shouldn't have tried to move the wagon," Charley said glancing at Father who nodded at him.

"That's okay. Now you get to wait on me hand and foot!" John said as he pulled a pocket dictionary from his new boots.

Charley picked up his boots and handed his orange to John. "You need this more than me," he said. He looked in the other boot and a silver flash caught his eye. A pocket knife. He looked at Father and smiled.

"Let's get to work, Charley. The cows won't milk themselves," Father said.

Arrowheads

Spring 1893

"John, get your nose out of your book. Mother said we had to feed the chickens. If you don't, I'm going to tell on you!" Nell said. John, leaning against the fence, peered over the top of his book, stuck out his tongue and flipped a page.

"Hey Nell, want to see a dead person?" John said.

"No!" Nell turned her back and flung more feed.

"Ah, come on. Don't be a chicken. Get it, 'chicken'," John said laughing.

Nell despised it when John call her that. She knew John was so proud of his new book about Egypt. She set the bucket down and stomped over to him.

"Oh, how can you look at that stuff," Nell said her blue eyes wide open, unable to leave the gruesome image of a mummified body.

"Did you know right here on our farm there's Indians buried?"

"You lie, John Herr! Father will whip you for that," Nell pointed at him.

"It's true," John said. He closed his book and limped towards the orchard patch. "Well, it could be true. Mr. Leap told me that there were Indians who lived right here long ago beyond the field we cleared last summer." John pointed west. "Mr. Leap said Nicholas

Yount, the man who sold Father and Mother the farm, found an arrowhead once."

"How's come Mother or Father never told us? Seems to me that would be something they would have told us IF it was true," Nell said, her hand on one hip.

"I don't know. Want to go look for some?" John said.

Nell considered it. It wasn't often her older brother willingly let her go along with him on one of his explorations. She was usually shooed to the cabin with Mother. Nell looked over at Mother who was hanging wash on the rail fence. Father and Charley were planting corn in the south field.

Nell used to have to run to keep up with John, but now she was able to keep pace with him as they crossed the field.

"Is it hurting much anymore?" Nell asked.

"Just when the weather changes. It kind of aches then," John said. They were careful not to step on the oats beginning to shoot from the soil. They heard a soft bark and looked over. It was Old Trail. He belonged to Mr. Benson, a neighbor.

"Do you think we'll find Indian bones, too?" Nell said softly, moving closer to John. She leaned down and pet Old Trail's scraggly coat.

"Nah, I don't want to go digging for Indian bones, but I do want to find some arrowheads."

They reached the spot Mr. Yount had told Mr. Leap about. It was between the corn and oat fields. A few trees lined the west end of the field.

John and Nell crouched down and began digging at the soft earth with hands and a small shovel John had brought with him.

After awhile Nell said, "How will I know if it's a flat rock or an arrowhead?"

"An arrowhead will be small, triangular shaped and pointed at one end. Remember the book I borrowed from Mr. Leap last year? It had pictures of arrowheads, Indian dress, and weapons."

Nell nodded and began digging again. They dug in silence for a long time. John was about to give up when he spotted a flat stone that looked like it had been pounded by something based on the markings. He wiped about the dirt that was crusted around it.

An arrowhead!

"I found one!" John yelled, holding it up in the air.

Nell shrieked and held it, touching the sharp point over and over. They continued digging. "Where's there's one there's bound to be more," John said.

"John, here's a couple more!"

They swept at the ground furiously. The arrowheads were only two inches below the top of the soil and there were at least four more.

"We did it! We hit the jackpot Nell!" John scooped up Nell and swung her around.

Old Trail sat up and gave a bark. "Real Indian arrowheads on our farm. I can't wait to tell Mr. Leap. Maybe he'll let me put some of them on display at his store."

They heard the clang-clang of Mother's dinner bell.

John and Nell filled their pockets and marked the spot of their discovery with a large field stone. They would come back for more excavating after dinner and chores.

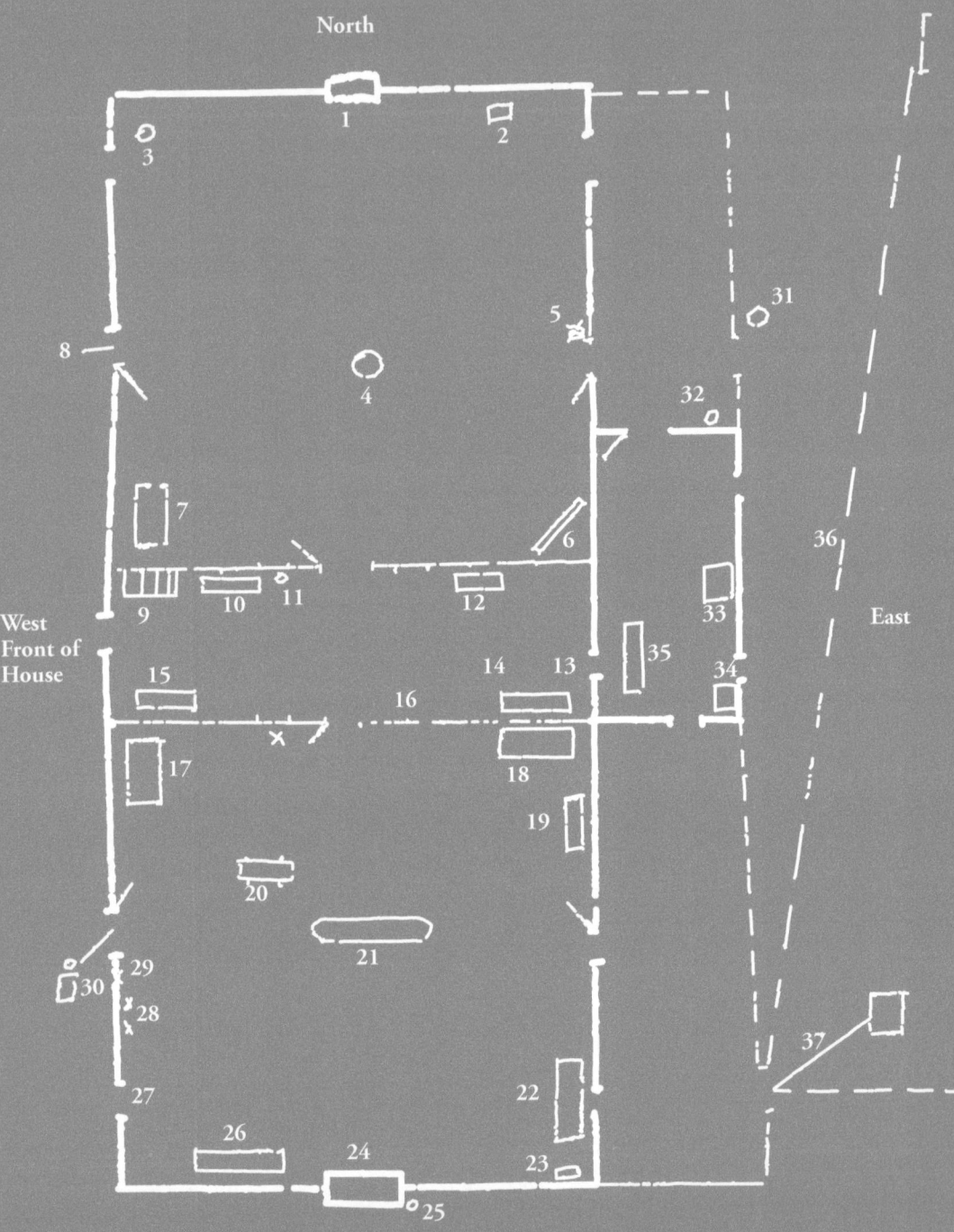

Drawing and key by Nell Herr Galey

Key to Drawing

1. Fireplace, where the baby sweeps cheeped and died
2. Mother's sewing machine
3. Round stand table; now in Remley's possession
4. Hanging lamp
5. Where cousin Alfred sat with the hair ribbon
6. Where the new organ was first placed
7. Bed where I had the earache
8. Door opening directly into yard. Flat rock used for step
9. Rough ladder-like steps leading to loft. Installed by father
10. Wooden wardrobe. Only closet we had. Moved to 39 in kitchen to make room for stairs
11. Where Charley hung me up in pa's pants
12. Bureau
13. Small, square window; mate for one on west
14. John's and Charley's bed
15. The 'trunnel' (trundle) bed
16. Dots around walls represent wooden pegs we hung cour clothes on
17. Bed
18. Mother's and Father's bed; my birthplace
19. Kitchen safe
20. Cradle. Place of my first memory
21. Dinner table
22. Cook stove
23. Kitchen stove woodbox
24. Fireplace
25. Slop bucket corner. In winter, bucket was kept in kitchen
26. Winter woodbox
27. Where Dick's cage hung from a beam
28. Where Nannie and I placed our chairs for Santa
29. Nail in wall where Nannie got her hair pulled out
30. To pump and milkhouse
31. Grapevine; where the accident happened
32. Where Mother sat and cried with toothache
33. Small summer kitchen cook stove
34. Small work table
35. Flour chest on which the spiced peach jar stood and from which Shirl and I swung from the beam above like monkeys
36. Path to woodhouse
37. Log to smoke house
38. Path to chicken lot and what have you
39. Entire house was weather boarded

SUMMER 1893

"Okay Nell, hold still. This is going to be fun," Charley said, lifting a pair of Father's work pants from a peg on the wall. Nell giggled as Charley helped her into the pants, picked her up and then hung her from a peg in the rafter above.

He gave her a gentle push and Nell swung from side-to-side. Laughing, she said, "Do it again!"

"Hang on, I'll be right back," Charley walked out of the bedroom, whistling. He shut the door behind him. Nell kicked trying to sway back and forth on her own. After a few seconds of this she turned and glanced out the window. Her smile faded like the quilt on

Mother and Father's bed. Charley was headed for the barn.

"Charley!" Nell shrieked. He didn't turn around. "Charley you get back here!"

Nell began kicking furiously and wiggling from side to side. She pushed herself up trying to free herself from Father's pants. It was no use.

Nell looked out the window once more. Charley was nowhere in sight. She began yelling at the top of her lungs. "Mother! I'm stuck!"

Mother, who was in the meat house on the east side of the cabin heard Nell's cries. She dropped the chicken she was plucking for dinner and ran for the cabin.

"What in the world?" She laughed when she saw Nell, red faced and squirming, in a pair of Father's pants hanging in the bedroom.

The tears poured over like a swollen creek bank, "Ch-Ch-Charley," Nell said, wiping her eyes. Mother lifted her out.

"I thought you were bit by a snake," Mother said smoothing her braids. "I thought you got bit by a snake or burned. You scared me have to death."

"Charley's a scoundrel. Just a scoundrel. Why does he hate me, Mother?"

"Oh Nell," Mother said, crouching in front of Nell. "He doesn't hate you. He teases you because he loves you. It's his way. Big brothers can be like that. You should be used to that by now."

"But why do I always trust him?" Nell asked.

"Because he's older and you should trust him. He'd do anything for you even though he'd never say it. He just likes to have fun every now and then."

"He's always picking on me," Nell said.

"Now you know that's not so. Remember last year when he killed that big black spider and put it in the wardrobe? And how I shrieked when I saw it? It had the thickest, fuzziest legs I've ever seen. I thought it was going to spring up and bite my leg. Charley just stood in the doorway and laughed," Mother shook her head, smiling. "And I laughed, too. He likes to joke around."

"But what if you hadn't heard me yelling?" Nell said.

Mother laughed, "Well, I guess you'd have hung in those pants a while longer."

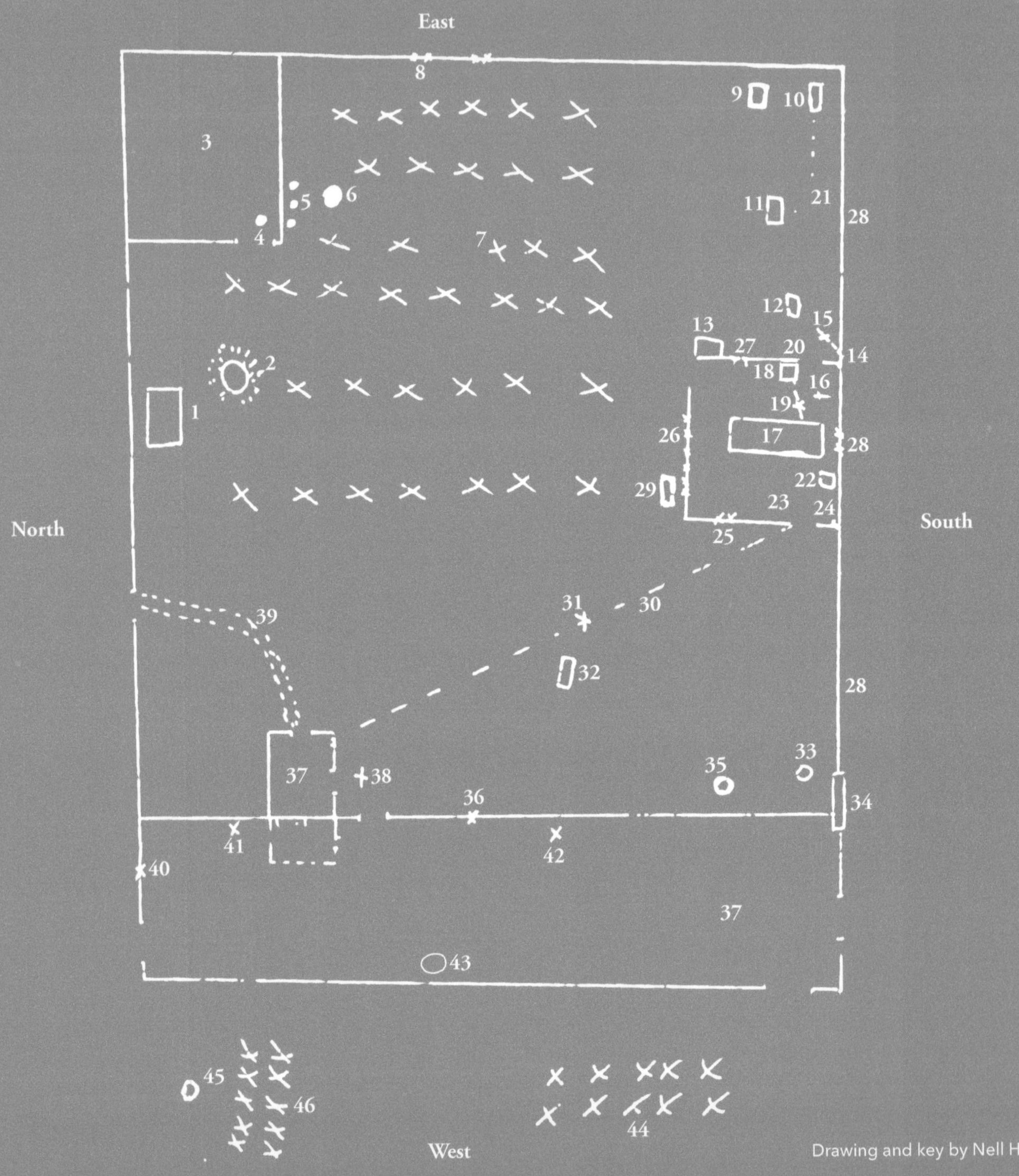

Drawing and key by Nell Herr Galey

Key to Drawing

1. Abandoned log stable
2. Apple tree. Ground beneath dumping place of dried up old shoes
3. Garden
4. Apple hole that I dug into
5. Bee gums
6. Bentover apple tree - my favorite playhouse regardless of bees
7. Orchard, old but well bearing
8. Rail fence
9. Log hen house; old; where I snagged my hand
10. Outhouse - where the mud dobbers built in the summer time
11. Small frame meat house
12. Ash hopper
13. Wood house
14. Huge walnut tree
15. Woodpile
16. Open air summer bathroom
17. Log house - where we lived
18. Log smoke house
19. Log walk to smoke house
20. Spot where fight over the churn took place; also whacking Nan's foot
21. Path to outhouse - and around
22. Small frame milkhouse
23. Wooden pump
24. Peach tree overhung with grapevine
25. A sort of smooth-rail fence
26. Rail fence
27. A kind of picket fence
28. Rail fence - all replaced with new picket fence later
29. Two frame rooms; later joined to log house, and still later to new frame house were used as summer kitchen and wood house
30. Path to barn from yard gate
31. Spot where Shirl encountered the rattlesnake
32. Small frame grainery
33. Wooden pump, supplying water to horse trough
34. Hollowed out log water trough
35. Walnut tree where each summer Nannie and I had our swing
36. Where Nannie and I had our 'slidin' board
37. Barn
38. Where little Fox gave me a bang with his hoof
39. Wagon drive to woods lane
40. Where cows were dehorned
41. Huge very old stump
42. Stump similar to above
43. Manure pile
44. Orchard father set out shortly after moving to new home
45. The 'no-good' pear tree
46. Blackberry and raspberry patch
47. Present day cow stable built on later

FALL 1893

The sky darkened to the west. Thunder rumbled overhead. A breeze picked up, slicing through the thick humid air ruffling Nell's work bonnet.

"Oh, that is delicious," Nell said lifting her face to the wind.

"I think it's going to be a fierce one," Mother said as she looked to the west. She bent down to cut another stalk of broccoli.

Nell was squatting behind her. She lifted a cabbage and beamed. "Look at this one. It's the best yet."

"We'll need it," Mother said, wiping at her brow. "The Farmer's Almanac is calling for a harsh winter."

More thunder growled. Nell shivered as goose bumps rose all over her arms. Boom! The ground shook sounding like a cannon had been fired in the woods. Nell jumped to Mother and they turned around. The wild wind was whipping the swing that hung from a walnut tree.

"We'll let Mother Nature do her work and come back to the garden later," Mother said. "Let's get inside and clean these."

Just then they heard shouts. Mother looked down the path to the barn. She grabbed Nell by the hand and ran.

"What's wrong? What's wrong!" Nell shouted.

Mother stopped at the gate and was working to unlatch it when Nell looked ahead.

The barn!

Flames poked from the roof and smoke rolled out the front doors. Nell could see John struggling to hold the reins of both Old Moll and Old Weasel. He was leading them up the path to the grainery.

"Where's Father and Charley?" Mother asked John when they reached him.

"Inside trying to put out the flames," John said, coughing. Mother pushed Nell at John. "You two stay here. Don't move. Hold the horses steady as best you can."

John and Nell watched as she disappeared into the barn. The smoke swallowing her. More shouts. A few second later, all three of them ran out. The flames and smoke had overcome them.

John and Nell tied the horses to a rail fence and ran to Father, Mother and Charley. As the wind and rain blew, the five of them stood watching the barn and their precious hay burn to the ground.

"Dang lightening," Charley said as he wiped the soot and smoke from his red eyes. "One crack and it wipes out all of our hay harvest in minutes. It's not fair!" He picked up a pail that had held water, a meager attempt to douse some flames, and threw it against the fence. "It's not fair I tell you."

"I know it's bad, son, but the most important thing is we're all okay," Father said putting a hand on his shoulder.

Charley's temper could flare up as quickly as the lightening. Anymore it seemed it was only Father who could calm him down. Now that he was eleven, Charley had outgrown Mother's soothing touches and would shrug them off. They watched as Charley walked off to the woods.

As fast as the storm had passed over them, it was gone. The fierce wind and rain left cool, damp air behind.

"I can't believe you two were in there," Mother said to Father. "You weren't going to save it." She looked at Father, who would not look her in the eye. "You should know better Benjamin Levi."

Father stared off to the woods watching Charley slip inside them. "I know it, Abigail, but we had to try. We work hard all summer cutting hay and we had to try. Otherwise, what kind of farmers would we be. We don't give up." Father looked down at her and put his arm around her waist. She swatted him away.

They turned at the sound of horses coming up the lane. It was Mr. Benson and his son who had a farm down the lane from them. Old Trail followed.

"What can we do for you, Ben? Abigail?" Mr. Benson said as he dismounted.

The Herr family had helped Mr. Benson put up a barn two seasons ago. His wife and baby daughter had died last winter of pneumonia. Mother often sent bread, pies, and pudding to them as well as vegetables from the garden.

"I may need some hay," Father said and gave a laugh at his sad joke.

"We'll get a new barn up in no time," Mr. Benson said. His son, Carl, nodded. "Tomorrow we can begin cutting the wood. I'll send word to the neighbors and get plenty of help. Leap said there's some young men over near Lebanon looking for work."

"Everyone has their crops to get in," said Father. "No time for barn building now. We can start after harvest."

Mother looked at Father, "But we'll be into December by then and..."

Mr. Benson stepped forward, "Now nonsense Ben. Just put that pride of yours away for now. Harvest being delayed a few days won't hurt none of us."

"Okay well tell them Lebanon folks I'll pay a good wage and we'll feed them, too. And we're paying you and any other neighbors that can help," said Father.

Mr. Benson waved this off.

"Thank you both," Mother said as Mr. Benson and Carl mounted their horses. Father shook their hands.

Nell, who had sat on the ground and was petting Old Trail. She felt less afraid now. Charley had returned from cooling off in the woods.

"Well let's get in and tomorrow we'll start cleaning up. Maybe there's some hay that survived the fire," Mother said.

"Let's get a good night's sleep," Father said. "Tomorrow we'll begin the fastest barn raising in Boone County."

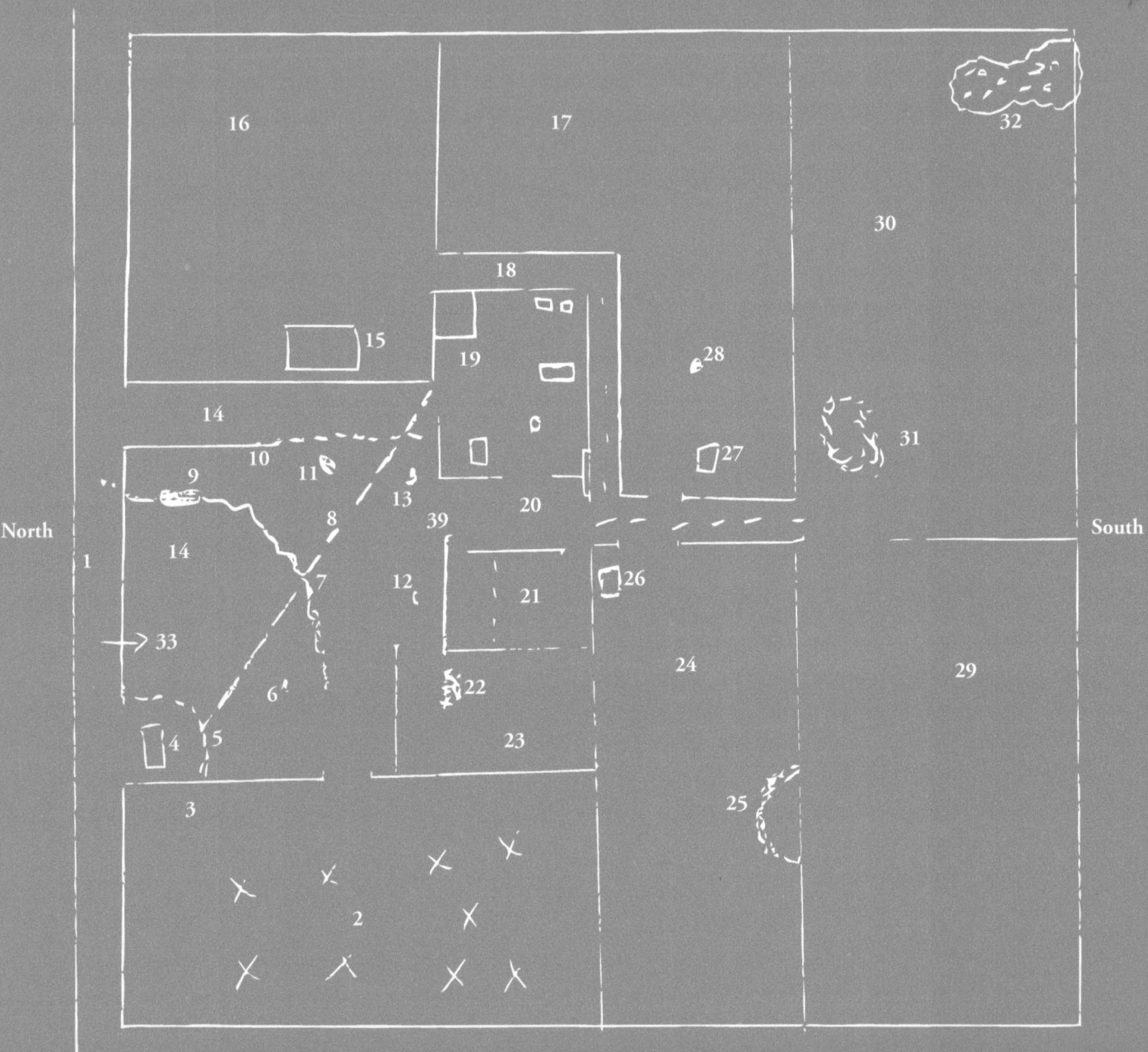

Drawing and key by Nell Herr Galey

Key to Drawing

1. Dirt road
2. Stumpy new ground
3. Funeral pyre of Old Trail (neighbor's dog)
4. School house
5. Rail fence
6. Spot of Shirl's planned fish pond
7. Small ditch
8. Path to School house
9. Where the iris grew
10. Mulberry tree
11. Hog 'waller'
12. Old Charley's grave – approximate location of
13. Walnut tree under which Nannie and I had our 'school fight'
14. Dirt lane
15. Where our 'new' house stands today
16. Cleared and smooth field
17. Field – very stumpy – plowshares broke on roots – Charley dynamited
18. Lane
19. House and barn premises
20. Cow lot
21. Orchard and berry patch set out by Father
22. Brush patch – where I went to Father about the snake
23. Bull lot, in woods
24. Cleared field
25. Site of supposed Indian camp – where John found arrow heads
26. Abandoned log cobin – one room, floorless lean-to
27. Cabin, duplicate of 26
28. Site of my terror
29. Field – a few trees at west end
30. Heavy woods
31. Pawpaw patch
32. Stagnant swamp criss-crossed with ancient fallen trees
33. Front pasture

WINTER 1893

Mother stood by the fire stirring oatmeal in the large, black kettle. She had one hand to her jaw and gave a small cry.

"Is your tooth bad again this morning?" Nell said as she dipped peaches from the jar into a bowl.

Mother nodded, wiping at her eyes. "This tooth has gone sour and I wish it would make up its mind to either stop hurting or fall out."

The east kitchen door opened and the boys stomped in from the cold.

"Father said he'll be awhile," John said. "The blacksmith from Fayette is here to re-shoe Old Moll."

"Must need a new shoe from banging Nell on the hind-end last week," Charley said, ruffly Nell's hair.

Nell stuck out her tongue at him. "It did hurt," she said. "Wonder why he did that? I give him sugar cubes."

"Maybe he was mad because he wanted more," John said as he bent over and rubbed at his leg.

"How's your leg today?" Mother said as she set down a bowl in front of him. Charley gave everyone a spoon.

"Better than yesterday. Aches a little, that's all," John said.

"It's this freezing weather," said Mother. "The only thing cold weather is good for is the winter wheat. I just wish you'd feel better son."

While the children ate, Mother picked up the small block of salt she had set near the fire. Wrapping it in a cloth, she held it against her jaw.

"Clean these dishes when you're finished, bring in more firewood and then go outside to play. I'm going to lie down and see if I can get this tooth to settle," Mother said walking into the bedroom.

"Yes ma'am," they said in unison.

The three of them sat in silence eating.

Nell said, "Want to build a snowman after chores? Or make snow angels?"

"Naw," John said. "I'm going to come in and read after we're done."

Nell watched Charley, who was finishing his third bowl of oatmeal. Charley pretended he didn't know Nell was staring at him.

"Want to do something?" she finally asked him.

Silence.

Nell was about to carry her bowl to the wash basin where John was cleaning up when Charley glanced at her and grinned. "I'm going to teach you to ice skate," Charley said. She shook her head.

"I'll call you scaredy-cat for the rest of your life if you don't go," Charley warned.

"I don't care," Nell said.

"Yes you do," Charley said. "I promise I'll hold your hand the entire time. I won't let go. It won't be like last time."

Nell looked him in the eye for a long minute. Charley's eyes told her he was being sincere this time.

"Okay. I'll go," Nell said.

The snow was past Nell's knees at times. She struggled to keep up with Charley's long strides. He had a pair of ice skates slung over each shoulder. They crossed through "Stump Field" where the trees had been cleared last year and the ground was uneven in places where roots and small stumps remained.

Nell tripped and fell to her knees. Charley walked back to her and helped her up. "I'm going to clean up this field for once and all this spring," Charley said.

"How are you going to do that?" Nell asked brushing the snow from her coat.

"I don't know yet. But I'll think of something," Charley said.

They headed toward the woods. The swamp was in the southeast corner. Charley and John had cleared off several fallen trees and made a skating area in the shallow part after Mother had told them they were not allowed to skate on the deep part.

No matter how cold it was, she was never satisfied the pond was frozen solid. The boys complained until Father took them aside and told them Mother had a cousin who drowned in a pond south of Fayette. Her name was Sarah and she was five years old. She was playing on the frozen pond and fell through the ice. All of this was enough to scare Nell and keep her in the shallow end. For a long time, she refused to skate and when she finally tried it, it was a disaster.

Nell sat on a log and put on her skates. "Make sure they're tight around the ankle. So one doesn't fall off like last time," Charley said recalling Nell tripping and skate flying. Nell refused to give skating another try.

"They're tight," Nell said. "Now help me up."

"You can stand up on your own," Charley said.

"I can't," Nell said.

"Yes, you can. Here, take my hand," Charley said. Nell tentatively reached for it. Charley pulled her up. "Let's go. We'll freeze if we don't get moving."

"Okay now keep hold of me with both your hands and look me in the eye. No, don't look down," Charley said. He gently pushed back and Nell half-skated, half-walked toward him.

"Good. Now relax and push your feet forward," Charley said.

"I feel like a newborn calf trying to find her legs," Nell laughed. But she was staying upright, skates on.

"You look like one, too," Charley said. "You're doing real good. Straighten up a bit."

Charley slid to the side of her and held onto one hand. Each time Nell looked down, Charley lifted her chin.

"You're getting it, Nelly," Charley said as they made a turn. He stopped and let go of her hand. She slid forward with a scream. Birds took flight from the woods.

"Charley! You told me you wouldn't let go!" Nell shrieked and laughed.

"Careful or you're bottom will be sore again," Charley said whizzing past her.

"I think I've got it," Nell beamed. She wobbled but stayed on her feet.

"Pretty soon you'll be able to skate backwards," Charley said and then he jumped over a log that he and John had placed there for this purpose. He made a perfect landing and turned back to Nell.

"Wow!" Nell said easing over to the end of the log and sitting down. "Do it again, Charley."

And Charley did.

Benjamin L. Herr

Abigail Herr and Charles Herr

John Herr

Spring 1894

"We've got enough dynamite to blow a hole to India," John said as he and Charley walked to Stump Field. Charley grinned at him.

"Someday I'm going there, you know," John said. "Want to go with me?" One of the latest books John was reading was a history of the Indian Empire.

"Why would you want to go that far? What's so great about India," Charley said, shifting the rolls of dynamite in his arms. The salmon-pink early morning sky cast a warm glow across the horizon.

"So I can see that," John stopped, nodding toward the new sun. "But in India."

"The sun's going to look the same over there," Charly said. He strode confidently over the bumpy ground. John slowed looking at the horizon.

"No it won't. Not to me anyway because I'll be on the other side of the world," John said.

They walked on in silence. When Charley reached a spot where a tree had been felled, he stopped. "I'll be darned if I'm going to break anymore plowshares in this field," Charley said.

"Does Mother know we're doing this?" John said as he helped his brother work a stick of dynamite in the ground.

"Naw, but she'll know soon enough," Charley laughed.

"You're going to scare the daylights out of her and Nell," John said but he was laughing, too.

"I'm just fooling. Father warned her yesterday," Charley said. "Nell wanted to come along but Mother needed her help."

"Do you think one will be enough?" John said as he handed his brother the wooden box of matches.

"We'll see. Depends on how deep and far the roots go," Charley said. "The old oak stump over there will probably take three."

"You hope it does," John smiled.

"You get going over that way," Charley signaled with a tilt of his head. "On the count of three, I'm going to light this and we'll need to run like bandits."

"How far should we go?" John said, beginning to limp off.

"Let's go to that small rise," Charley said. As John headed for it, Charley struck the match. One the first try, the dynamite lit. Charley scooped up the remaining sticks and ran for John. He settled down next to him. The brothers lay on their bellies in the dirt, hats down low over their eyes. One second went by. Then two. Then three.

"Well spit on a frog," Charley said, sitting up. "I don't think it took."

He and John stood and Charley headed toward the dynamite. "You wait here," Charley turned and told John who was a few feet behind him. As Charley cautiously walked back to the dynamite he was halfway there when "Kaboom!"

Charley and John both hit the dirt face down. The ground trembled and soft, black dirt rained down on Charley.

John lifted his head and called to Charley, "I think it took." The brothers laughed and agreed not to tell Mother about this.

Original cabin location

Summer 1894

Charley, John and Nell walked down the dirt lane that led to the cabin and headed west. Mother was in there lying down. The baby was due in four months, November, and Mother felt sick most of the day. She laughed it off saying this child would surely have a full head of hair.

Father had started building the new house. It was going up straight north of the cabin. It would be a palace compared to the cabin – two stories, ten rooms, and a wide front porch. The children could hardly wait; it meant they would have their own bedrooms.

Supervising the farm fell on Charley's shoulders now that Father was busy with the house. And Charley relished being in charge.

Today Charley was scouting for stumps in the new field Father had just bought. He would begin dynamiting them in the afternoon. John was planning a small fish pond in the low swampy ground next to the small ditch that arced around the cow pasture. He even brought pencil and paper to sketch a design. Nell was along to help.

Charley left John and Nell and walked on to the field ahead. As he walked along the edge of the land toward the bull lot at the edge of the woods, he heard Nell scream. He turned and ran back.

The ditch was notorious for snakes. Most non-poisonous but you never knew. Nell was like a magnet for snakes, Charley thought as he raced to her, half angry that she interrupted his scouting. Just yesterday she had come to him and Father as they were burning brush complaining about a snake in the milkhouse. It ended up being a puny garden snake.

John and Nell were sitting down looking at something in the tall grass. Nell was bawling.

"What happened? Were you bit?" Charley said when he reached them. He looked down and fell silent. He saw what they were seeing.

Old Trail.

He was lying on his side as still as a wood post.

"Why'd he have to die?" Nell wailed, resting her head on Old Trail's.

"Hey, he was old Nellie," Charley said crouching next to her.

"Yes Nell," John said. "Mr. Benson told me once he didn't know his age because he just showed up on their farm one day as a young dog. He's had him forever. Even before Charley was born."

Nell wiped at her eyes and lay down next to Old Trail. "Maybe a dog will show up here someday," Charley said.

"I hope so. I want a new puppy so I can have it for a long, long time," Nell said.

"Mr. Leap's always getting dogs hanging around the store for scraps. We can ask him next time we're in Fayette."

Nodded her head.

"What do we do with Old Trail? We have to tell Mr. Benson. We can't leave him lying out here like this," Nell said, shooing a fly away.

"We'll bury him. Mr. Benson won't mind him being buried on our place. Half the time he was here anyway," said John. John and Charley looked around for a good spot; a place Old Trail liked to investigate.

"Under that tree," Charley said pointing to the corner where the pasture met the new field. "Old Trail liked it under that big tulip tree in the shade."

"I'll run and get a shovel. There's one at the bull lot," Charley said. "But first help me move him."

Charley and John gently lifted Old Trail and carried him under the tree. The wind shifted and a gentle breeze ruffled the leaves above. While Charley left to get the shovel, Nell and John gathered flowers for the grave.

After Charley tossed the last shovel full of dirt on Old Trail's grave, he stood back and watched as Nell placed flowers on the grave. John had found a round field stone to use as a marker.

"We have to say something. We can't just bury him and leave," Nell said.

"Let's say what we liked about him," John offered.

They were quiet for a moment. The tree branches creaked above them. A few cows were hanging their heads over the split-rail fence watching.

"I liked his soft fur," Nell said.

"His fur was raggedy and full of burrs," Charley said.

"Shhhhh," John elbowed him.

"I liked it anyway. He liked it when I pet him and got the burrs out," Nell said.

"He always seemed to understand what I was saying when I talked to him," John said. John and Nell looked over at Charley.

"He was a good companion," Charley said as he knelt down, touched the grave, and wiped a tear onto his sleeve.

New 10-room house

Fall 1894

John, Charley, and Father shucked the last row of corn for the evening. It had been an unseasonably warm fall and this November evening was no exception.

Charley took off his hat and wiped his brow with his sleeve. This was the last load of the day and he was glad. His stomach was, too. It started growling for supper an hour ago.

John and Charley would take his wagon load of corn to the feed mill tomorrow where it would be ground as feed for the cows, horses, pigs and chickens.

"Get going," Charley said and whistled at Old Moll.

"How's Mother feeling?" John asked Father. He had been checking on her every few hours that day.

"Fine. This one is taking its time, though," Father said. "But I think you'll have a brother or sister by morning."

"Good thing we moved into the new house last week," John said.

"That's probably what helped this little one along. We weren't expecting this until the end of the month," Father said. A worried look passed over his face.

"She'll be fine. She always is," Charley said. "She'll be playing her organ next week." He rubbed at his shoulder. Last week they had picked up Mother's organ at Mr. Leap's store. He pulled a muscle lifting it.

The organ was a beautiful, gleaming cabinet model from Moline, Illinois. It was a birthday present from Father. She had always wanted one and now with the new house they had the perfect place for it in the front parlor.

When they walked into the kitchen Nell was bustling around. She ordered them to sit at the table and then checked their hands to make sure they'd washed.

"Well, aren't you the little mother," Father said. He kissed Nell on the top of her head and went upstairs to check on Mother.

Mrs. Leap had come to help Mother with the baby. And, of course, Nell would help as well.

"What did you fix for us?" Charley said to Nell.

"Biscuits, stew and a pie," Nell said, setting their plates in front of them. "Isn't it exciting this baby will be the first born in our new house!"

"Sure Nell," John said, stuffing his mouth.

"Mmmmmmm. This is better than Mother's," Charley said.

"Really?" Nell said, smiling.

"Yes, ma'am. Would I lie to you?" Charley said.

"Yes. Yes, you would," Nell said. She swatted him with her apron.

The next morning before dawn the Herr children woke to the squeaks and squalls of the baby's cries. The scrambled out of bed and ran to Mother and Father's room.

Father was sitting at the edge of the bed cradling a bundle in his arms. Mother looked exhausted but was beaming and held out her hand.

"Come say hello to your new brother, Ben."

Enrichment Questions/ Activities for Students

1. The story ends with the birth of Ben Herr. What happens next for the family and the farm?

2. Over the years the Herr children and heirs found Native American arrowheads on the farm. Which Native American tribes lived in Boone County, Indiana or the Midwest region? Research and create a visual project, give an oral report, or write a paper about your research.

3. Research farming practices in Indiana or the Midwest the 1800s. What was life like for farmers and their families? How has farming changed?

4. Consider what the benefits and drawbacks to living on a farm. Would you like or dislike farm life?

5. Delve into the architecture of log cabins. What materials were needed in the 1800s? How were they built? Build your own miniature log cabin.

6. Research the role of women who farmed in the 1800s. What was it like to live, work, and raise a family during this time?

www.ingramcontent.com/pod-product-compliance
Lightning Source LLC
Chambersburg PA
CBHW042130040426
42450CB00003B/138